MOTHER'S DAY BOUQUET

MOTHER'S DAY ROSES, VIOLETS AND ANTIQUE LACE ON PAPER CRAFTS FOR CARDS, GIFTS AND DÉCOR

EASY PRE-PRINTED PAPER CRAFTS TO CUT, GLUE AND MAKE

The Anni Arts printable crafts are now in this easy and ready-to-craft format.
'Print-on-demand' makes printing as environmentally friendly as printing the crafts at home.

PROJECTS

SEE THE EQUIPMENT GUIDE, TIPS AND GENERAL INSTRUCTIONS ON THE FOLLOWING PAGE
SEE CUP CARD INSTRUCTIONS PLUS CHOC WRAPPER TIPS ON THE LAST TWO PAGES
ALL PAGES HAVE THE RELEVANT INSTRUCTIONS PRINTED WITH THE PAPER CRAFT ITEM

GREETING CARDS

SHAPED STAND-UP TEACUP CRADLE CARD WITH BACK STAND – on front and back covers
TWO-PART ENVELOPE FOR THE CUP CARD – with a 'stamp' for a hand-delivered card
TEA BAG PACKET TO ADD TO THE TEACUP CARD AS A LITTLE FAVOUR
4" x 6" PHOTO APERTURE POSTCARD TOPPER, OR A CARD THAT FOLDS TO 4"x6"
LACY CROCHET ENVELOPE FOR THE 4" x 6" PHOTO APERTURE CARD
Download free blank templates for a 4"x6" and 5" x 7"card to print

PAPER CRAFTS AND PACKS

SERVIETTE RING – add to a cloth or paper serviette to present along with the cupcake
CUPCAKE WRAP AND TOPPERS – *Download additional printable cupcake wrappers in the freebie file*
GIFT BAG FOR A GIFT OR CHOCOLATES – use with included handles or ribbon
TEA TOTE GIFT BAG FILLED WITH TEABAGS IN ENVELOPES – add ribbon handles
GIFT CARD ENVELOPE – fits a credit card-sized store gift card
SCENT SACHET – add potpourri for a fragrant drawer sachet or bath salts for a nice soak
LACE PATCHWORK CHOCOLATE WRAPPER FOR A LARGE SLAB - *See wrap and trim ideas at the back*
SMALL CHOCOLATE WRAPPER FOR A SNACK CHOCOLATE OR HERSHEY BAR
GIFT TAG ASSORTMENT AND BOOK MARK – on the covers
ASSORTED LABELS, ENVELOPE SEALS AND SENTIMENT STRIPS – plus extra bits to use with the paper crafts
GIFT WRAP – for a small gift like a bar of soap, candles and such
ITTY BITTY GIFT BAG – for a small item like a charm bracelet, locket, brooch or lipstick
PILLOW PACK – make it in a snap for a small gift box

DÉCOR

PRETTY BOOT WITH GIFT CARD POCKET – to hang over a door or drawer knob
BUNTING – lace flags to use as décor on a wall, above a table, over a door or in a window
TIE-ON WINE OR BEVERAGE LABEL – a label that is tied over the bottle's own label

FREE EXTRAS *Download additional items to print at:* ANNI ARTS www.anniarts.com/mothersday-clip-art
ALSO SEE *Mother's Day printable crafts as downloads from* ANNI ARTS CRAFTS *at* www.anniartscrafts.com

The Anni Arts **Mother's Day Bouquet** images are also on pretty, ready-to-buy products like mugs, tea pots, chocolate boxes, beverage labels, compacts, cakes, phone cases and more! ANNI ARTS www.anniarts.com

For these projects I used my own drawings of roses and violets and combined them with lace and embroidery engravings from antique books. The antique images are not in perfect condition, but that adds to their charm. I kept the worn look of the engravings and only did minimal restoration of the images – then added soft colours.

EQUIPMENT

SCISSORS small and sharp for detail and large for cutting the craft pages from the book
CRAFT KNIFE with a sharp blade to cut straight lines (optional)
RULER with a metal edge if used with a craft knife
GLUE STICK
ADHESIVE TAPE as an alternative to glue on some items. Double-sided tape is best, as it can be concealed.
PAPER SCORER

A paper scorer is an instrument to draw a line to make folding that line easier.
It makes a dent on the card or paper, but does not cut right through. It is essential for creating tidy and precise paper crafts. Craft shops sell special scoring instruments, but an empty ballpoint pen is just as efficient – and is my personal favorite! You can also use the blunt side of the blade of a craft knife to make a *very light* score. And in a pinch you can also use a butter knife (with no serrations on the blade).
Note: When scoring regular paper like that on **the pages in this Cut-N-Make book**, take care to *score lightly* – the paper can easily tear if the score runs too deep. However, items on the **covers** *do need deep scores*.

TIPS AND GENERAL INSTRUCTIONS

All pages have the relevant instructions printed with the paper craft item. Also see the specific instructions for the cup card and other items, as well as ideas for the chocolate wrappers, on the last two pages.

TIPS:

First cut each craft page from the book along the guide line.
Then score all lines as indicated.
Cut out the shape of the pre-printed card element or paper craft item.
Fold on the scored lines and glue as indicated.
Add labels, seals and tags as desired. Also use the extra items for additional crafts or more detail.
Keep the page from which the item was cut until the item is complete - to refer to instructions on the page.

GREETING CARDS:

Make sure that glue goes all the way to the edges of the card elements. Lay a blank piece of paper over a freshly positioned and glued element and glide the edge of a ruler over the covered section to flatten and properly glue the element to the underlying layer. The cover paper protects the glued elements.

The aperture *card/ postcard* needs to be constructed from *cardstock*, as the paper in this book is not heavy enough for a card base. It is glued to the blank card cut from cardstock. Cut a card base to the dimensions given below, or *download the printable blank templates and print* the card base on printable cardstock from Anni Arts at **www.anniarts.com/mothersday-clip-art**

Cut a **10" x 7" (approx. 25.5 x17.75 cm)** *backing for a card that folds to* **5"x 7"**. *Or cut 5" x 7" for a postcard.*
Cut a **8" x 6" (approx. 20 x 15 cm)** *backing for a card that folds to* **4" x 6"**. *Or cut 4" x 6" for a postcard.*
Score through the middle to fold the card and add the cardmaking elements to the front.

SEE THE GROWING LIST OF ANNI ARTS CUT-N-MAKE BOOK TITLES – CHECK www.anniarts.com FOR UPDATES!

ANNI ARTS
CUT-N-MAKE
BOOKS

EASTER DAFFODILS
TULIPS & EASTER EGGS
REINDEER TOILE DE JOUY
SCANDINAVIAN CHRISTMAS

Optional
paper handles

Punch holes for a ribbon handle and add a tag.
Choose a label to add to back of packet(optional)

Score

D

Punch holes for ribbon handle

Tab 3
Glue to the score line.

Score -   –

Tab 2   Glue on top to line
Fold under Tab 3

Score -

Score to dot

Glue

C

Score

Score

Glue

Cut just inside all outlines

Glue

Score

Glue

Score

Glue

Put teabag in tea envelope
Glue top flap to seal packet

Optional
paper handles

Place tea envelopes in tote

Score

B

Punch holes for ribbon handle

Uppermost tab. Do NOT glue as it adheres to the top of tab 3

Tab 1

ANNI ARTS

Score to dot

Score -   –

Tab 2   Glue on top to line
Fold under Tab 3

Score -

Glue

A

Cut just inside all outlines

Score

Score

Glue

Glue

Glue

Glue

Score

Score

Score

Put teabag in tea envelope
Glue top flap to seal packet

Cut just inside all outlines

Score

Glue

Score

Glue

Glue

Envelope
Seals

Glue

Score

Carefully cut to separate the tea envelopes
TEA ENVELOPES 3,4 and 5
Score and fold like 1 and 2

Glue

Glue

Score

Glue

Glue

Score

Score

Glue

Glue

Put teabag in tea envelope
Glue top flap to seal packet

Score

Glue

Score

Glue

TEACUP CRADLE CARD ENVELOPE FRONT
Cut inside the lines for a white bleed edge. You can also use decorative edge scissors on top flap
Fold side tabs back after scoring and glue to envelope back

Happy
MOTHER'S DAY

'Stamp' for envelope for 4x6" card

Shape cut —

Optional butterfly layer for envelope. Front or back.
Glue only body for lifted wings. Score on lines.

Score -

Score -
and
fold

-

-

Glue

Glue

Score -
and
fold

Score -
and
fold

Score
and
fold

Glue

HEART PACKET/ ENVELOPE

Punch holes for a ribbon tie
or seal with one of the
extra elements in the book.

Fits a *Lindt Coeur Fin*
chocolate heart
or small sweetie
or truffle

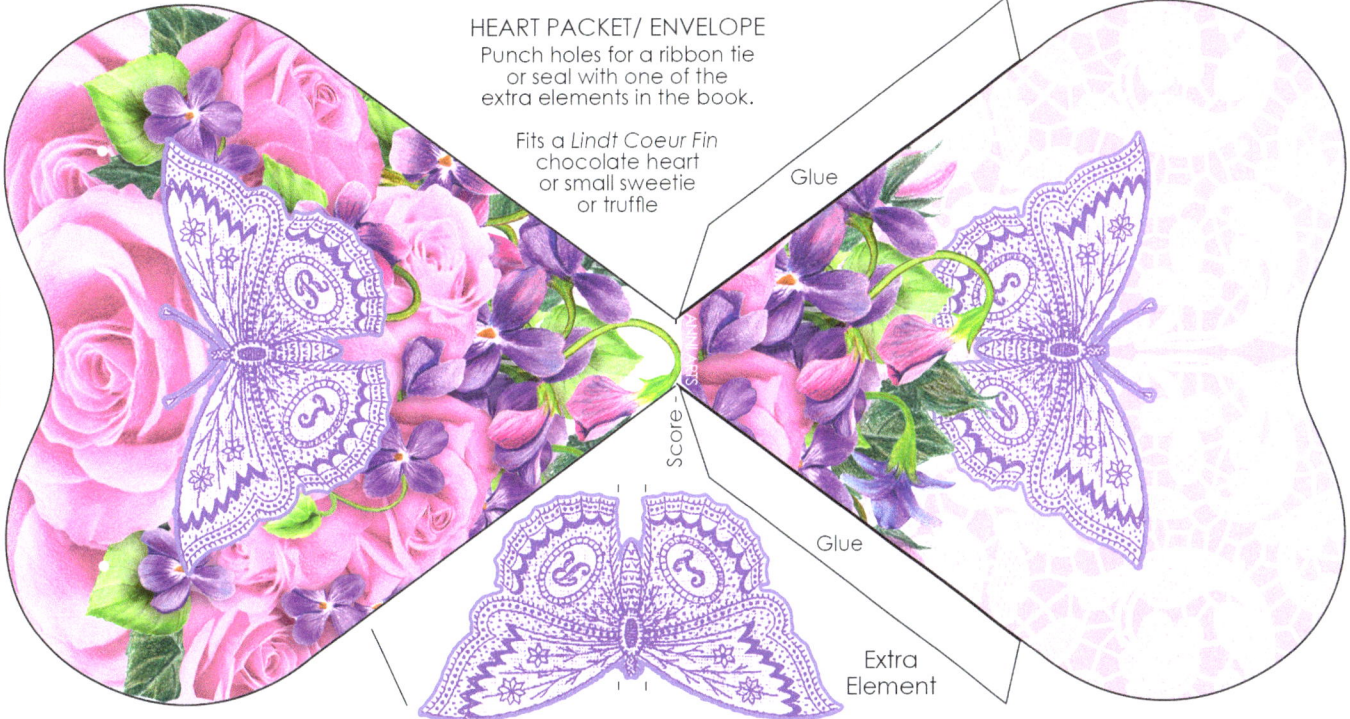

Glue

Glue

Hole Guides

Score

Extra
Element

Optional butterfly layer for envelope. Front or back.
Glue only body for lifted wings. Score on lines.

Cut

TEACUP CRADLE CARD ENVELOPE BACK

Cut bunting flags just inside of the outline.
The edges can also be cut with decorative scissors. Punch holes
Fold back reinforcement flaps. Glue to flag base.
Wait till glue is dry before punching holes through
both layers. Thread ribbon through holes by
threading under flag and over corners

Extra element

Score

Score -

Extra elements

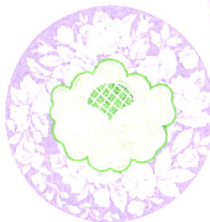

BUNTING/ FLAGS/ PENNANTS

Cut bunting flags just inside of the outline.
The edges can also be cut with decorative scissors. Punch holes
Fold back reinforcement flaps. Glue to flag base.
Wait till glue is dry before punching holes through
both layers. Thread ribbon through holes by
threading under flag and over corners

Extra element

Score

Score

Extra elements

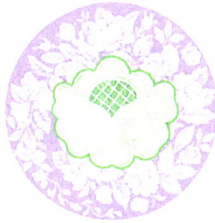

'Stamp' for envelope for 4x6" card

Optional butterfly layer for front of sachet
Score on lines and glue on body only

Optional back label for sachet

Optional rose layer for above bow on front of sachet

LOVE YOU

Optional strip seal for back of sachet

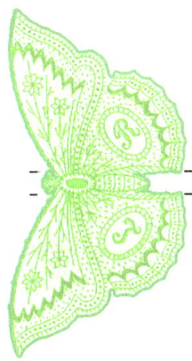

SCENT SACHET

ANNI ARTS

Score -

Score -

Score -

Score -

Glue or tuck in

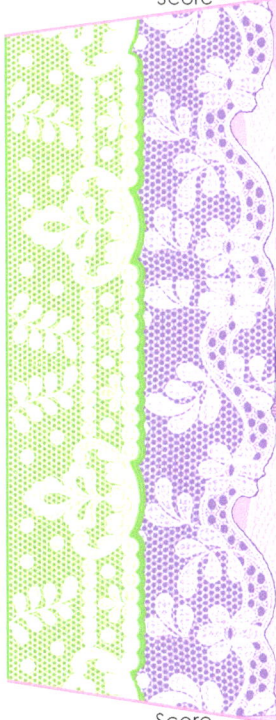

Glue

Glue

GIFT BAG BACK AND HANDLE. Glue handle at arrow positions. Glue side D to A of front section

C

D

glue

GIFT BAG HANDLE 2 (or use ribbon)

score -

score -

score -

Tab 1
Glue on top to line
Fold under Tab 3

Tab 3 Glue to the score line. Fold over tabs 1 and 2. Fold under Tab 1

Optional sentiments

GIFT BAG FRONT AND HANDLE. Glue handle at arrow positions. Glue side B to C of back section

A

B

glue

score

GIFT BAG HANDLE 1 (or use ribbon)

score

Tab 2
Glue on top to line
Fold under Tab 3

score

Tab1 Uppermost tab. Do NOT glue as it adheres to the top of tab 3

GIFT BAG STRIP SEAL - glue over edges of bag from front to back

ANNI ARTS

Top Layer

HAPPY MOTHER'S DAY   HAPPY MOTHER'S DAY

Hole for ribbon -

Front is slightly larger than back. Trim after gluing

Optional butterfly layer
Glue only body for lifted wings. Score on lines

BOOT WITH GIFT CARD POCKET
FRONT

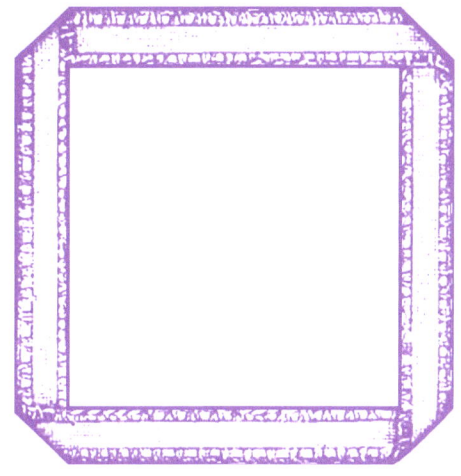

EXTRA LABELS

OPTIONAL BOOT LAYERS

✂

Happy
MOTHER'S
DAY

Envelope
Seal

White area forms
a pocket.
Do **not** glue

Gift card peeps from boot

Glue
to back
of boot
front

Score -

Glue up to line and along sides

BOOT WITH GIFT CARD POCKET
BACK

Glue

Glue

Glue grey area
and glue to back
of boot front

Score -

Score

Score

Tuck in
or Glue

4" x 6" PHOTO APERTURE CARD TOPPER OR POSTCARD

Cut away white area and place over a photo.
Cut a 4" x 6" backing for a postcard or download
and print a card on cardstock from
www.anniarts.com/

Cut away
Place over
photo

Score
from
dot to
dot

Score as
indicated

TIE-ON WINE/ BEVERAGE LABEL
Punch holes in corner tabs once tabs have been folded back and glued

Glue

Glue

Glue

Glue

Label with side reinforcement tabs.
Score sides and across corners. Fold all flaps back. Glue **under side** of flaps

ENVELOPE FOR 4 x 6'' CARD

Glue

Fold back and glue

Score

Score

Glue

Glue

Score and fold

Score and fold

Fold back glued tabs

FRONT

Glue back to glued and folded tabs of front section

BACK

Score

Score

Score

ANNI ARTS

TEABAG PACKET FOR CRADLE TEACUP CARD

Score grey lines and fold. Glue side tab and bottom tab to make packet.
Place teabag in packet, place teabag string through top and glue and close top.

Score - across tab

Score - across tabs

Glue

Punch hole

Thanks
MOM

Optional
back label

Thanks
MUM

Score -

Score -

Score -

Score and fold tag and glue over the tea tag
that is attached to the teabag you are using.

CUPCAKE TOPPERS

Glue toppers
back to back over
a toothpick and
insert into
cupcake

Score and
fold here.

Optional butterfly layer for front of cupcake
Glue only body for lifted wings. Score on lines.

CUPCAKE
WRAPPER

SERVIETTE RING

Extra mini flags for use on a
layer cake or card

M
O
M

M
U
M

Choose
MOM or
MUM

SERVIETTE RING TOPPER

ITTY
BITTY
GIFT
BAG

ANNI ARTS

Glue   Cut to line   Do not glue   Cut to line   Glue   Cut to line   Glue on under side

---

TEACUP CRADLE CARD INSTRUCTIONS. Use the teabag packet as a nice little card-n-gift set.

2
Flip card around.
The daffodil and egg is
on the back of the
finished card

3
Glue top tab up to
scored and folded line

4
Place back section behind front of card
and line up the edges of the cup shape

5
Optional:
Glue the teabag packet on
the inside below the top tab

1
Score –
and
make
a fold

Glue

Glue on
under side

Make a
small cut in
the rim of
the cup for
the egg
tag

Put
tea
tag
string
through
the cut
in rim

Fill the teabag packet with a teabag and replace the teabag tag with the egg tag

---

TIP: Include the white edges of the
book's page beyond the
gingham pattern for gift
wrap with a maximum
size to fully wrap
a large choc
bar

CHOCOLATE   WRAPPER IDEAS

1
A chocolate slab
with the wrapper edges
flattened and glued for a
modern "crimped" edge look

2
Wrap
the chocolate
in tissue paper first,
then trim the wrapper
so the tissue edges show

3
The
chocolate
wrapper used like
regular gift wrap to fully
wrap the slab. See TIP

4
The full
wrapper
trimmed for
a smaller
choc

4
Make
a sleeve
from the wrap
for a small snack
choc by gluing and
flattening the edges.
Glue the long back seam.
Glue one edge. Flatten.
Insert the chocolate. Glue
and flatten the other edge.

For the tie-on wine label, thread ribbon over the first edge, behind the label and over the second edge. Do to both the top and bottom using two lengths of ribbon. Tie with bows at the back.
A tag can be threaded in with the ribbon or be tied around the neck of the bottle.

The tag of the teabag is glued over the tag that comes with the teabag.

TIP: SHAKE the tealeaves in the teabag to distribute them evenly before placing it in the packet

Use the extra mini flags as bunting on a layer cake. Use skewers or drinking straws as flag 'poles'.Tie string from pole to pole. Glue flags over string. Tidy end points with bows. Choose MOM or MUM spelling for the flags.

Also see printable crafts with the Mother's Day theme

www.anniartscrafts.com

Contact Anni at www.anniarts.com